YESHIVA
OF THE
TELSHE ALUMNI

The Yeshiva of the Telshe Alumni
Torah's Way Station in Riverdale

Something unique is happening in Riverdale. In a secluded, suburban setting, so near and yet so far from the heart of New York, the YESHIVA OF THE TELSHE ALUMNI is writing a splendid chapter in the story of Torah education in America.

Come see for yourself.

You'll be greeted and made welcome by the students. They'll bring you a chair, offer you a *siddur*, ask how they can help. You'll see a staff of profound, dedicated *Roshei Yeshiva* who represent the finest products of American and Israeli *yeshivos*. You'll see these educators guiding their students from early in the morning until late—very late—at night. You'll see classes that are not permitted to grow to a size that would inhibit this personal relationship. You'll see an individual student discussing a personal problem with his *rebbe* or the *Rosh Yeshiva* without fear or embarrassment. You'll see groups of physicians or professionals and business people from the community coming for their regular *shiur* in the Yeshiva. You'll see the cleanliness and order, and you'll feel the sense of mission that permeates the entire Institution.

When a group of Telshe alumni set out and founded the Yeshiva several years ago, they had a few very clear goals: engage highly qualified *Roshei Yeshiva* and put them in charge; instill the historic Telshe tradition of dignity, order, idealism and absolute devotion to the needs of each student; and let the Yeshiva become a concerned, contributing part of the local Jewish community. They received the blessing of Harav Mordechai Gifter, who urged them to proceed and create a vibrant, independent institution that would bring pride to its roots in Telshe.

Such goals are gratifying. Even more heartwarming is that they are being realized! So much so that there are many more applicants than the Yeshiva can accommodate.

Seldom are expectations so well rewarded. That is why your much-needed support of YTA will accomplish so much.

MENORAS HAMAOR

The Days of Awe

MENORAS HAMAOR

The Days of Awe

RABBEINU YITZCHAK ABOHAV

Translated by
RABBI YAAKOV YOSEF REINMAN

C·I·S

P·U·B·L·I·S·H·E·R·S

New York · London · Jerusalem

ISBN 1-56062-041-2

Published and distributed
in the U.S., Canada and overseas by
C.I.S. Publishers and Distributors
180 Park Avenue, Lakewood, New Jersey 08701
(201) 905-3000 Fax: (201) 367-6666

Published in conjuction with
Yeshiva of the Telshe Alumni
4904 Independence Avenue
Riverdale, New York 10471

Distributed in Israel by
C.I.S. International (Israel)
Rechov Mishkalov 18
Har Nof, Jerusalem
Tel: 02-538-935

Distributed in the U.K. and Europe by
C.I.S. International (U.K.)
1 Palm Court, Queen Elizabeth Walk
London, England N16
Tel: 01-809-3723

Cover design by Ronda Kruger Israel

PRINTED IN THE UNITED STATES OF AMERICA

Table of Contents

Translator's Foreword

The Days of Awe is an excerpt from *Menoras Hamaor*, one of the great classics of Jewish religious literature. *Menoras Hamaor* consists of seven separate and distinct works, each dealing with a separate and distinct area of Jewish thought—the seven branches of the Menorah.

For centuries, *Menoras Hamaor* has enjoyed spectacular popularity. It has appeared in seventy-nine editions and has been translated into Ladino, German and Yiddish. First printed in Constantinople in 1514, it has since been reprinted in many cities on four continents.

As its basic premise, *Menoras Hamaor* uses the verse, "Turn away from evil and do good, search out peace and pursue it" (*Tehillim* 34:15). Drawing on the chronicles and timeless wisdom of the Agadic portion of the Talmud and on the Midrashim, it develops a system for the inprovement of the individual and the fulfillment of his role in society.

This volume, *The Days of Awe*, is an annotated excerpt from *The Light of Teshuvah*, the Fifth Light of the Menorah. It is an in-depth look at the ten day period beginning with Rosh Hashanah and climaxing with Yom Kippur. It directs the reader to the symbolism and meaning of this period and how it is meant to bring a person closer to Hashem.

The other Lights of the Menorah include: *The Light of Contentment, The Light of Expression, The Light of Mitzvos, The Light of Torah, The Light of Harmony,* and *The Light of Humility.*

The Days of Awe, an arrangement of a selection of chapters from *The Light of Teshuvah,* the Fifth Light of the Menorah, appears in the complete work as Section II, Chapters 1-8. This excerpt discusses the proper attitude one should have during the The Days of Awe, beginning with the preparations from as early as Rosh Chodesh of the month of Elul. The chapters dealing with Rosh Hashanah focus on its being the day of judgment, a time when it is crucial that one do teshuvah, and show how this date is particularly appropriate for this purpose from a historical viewpoint. They then tackle the perplexing paradox of the righteous person who suffers while the sinful one prospers. They conclude with a description of the relationship between the blowing of the shofar and teshuvah, followed by a comprehensive listing of the symbolism of the mitzvah of shofar.

The chapters dealing with Yom Kippur differentiate between those sins for which Yom Kippur atones and those for which it does not, outlining what one must do in order to enter Yom Kippur cleansed and pure. They then go on to describe the singular nature of this day—a day that is at once joyous and terrifying, a day of fasting that must be honored with holiday finery—and how it is designed to inspire a person to do teshuvah.

About the Author

The Abohav family was a very prominent family of outstanding scholars who lived in the Middle Ages. After the expulsion of the Jews from Spain, in 1492, branches of the family were established in North Africa, Turkey, Italy, and the Marrano communities of Northern Europe.

The life of the author, Rabbeinu Yitzchak Abohav, is shrouded in mystery, with very few details available. It is generally accepted that he lived in Spain in the latter half of the fourteenth century. His father, Rabbeinu Avraham Abohav, was quite possibly the Rabbeinu Yitzchak Abohav to whom Rabbeinu Yehudah ben Asher of Toledo, the son of the R'ash, addressed responsa in *Zichron Yehudah*.

The author's fame rests entirely upon his authorship of *Menoras Hamaor*, which is but one part of a trilogy. The other parts of the trilogy, *Aron Ha'edus* and *Shulchan Haponim* have been lost. The author describes all three parts of the trilogy, and their interrelationship, in the "Ode to the Menorah" (see Appendix A to *The Light of Contentment*, the First Light of the Menorah).

The little that is known about the author's life must be gleaned from what he himself writes in the introductpry "Ode to the Menorah" and "Profile of the Menorah" (see Appendix B to *The Light of Contentment*, the First Light of the Menorah). In "Profile of the Menorah", the author writes that a substantial part of his life was devoted to secular affairs. It was in his later years that he turned to writing and the rabbinate. He implies that part of his motivation for writing *Menoras Hamaor* was to have a systematic arrangement of the Agada to draw upon when he had to speak before the people. There is also a tantalizing reference in the "Ode to the Menorah", Part V, to some time spent in captivity. However, this might only be an allegorical allusion to the time he spent in secular pursuits.

Rabbeinu Yitzchak Abohav II, a descendant of the author who lived one hundred years later and died in 1493, was known as "the last gaon of Castille". He studied with Rabbeinu Yitzchak Canpanton and became the head of the Toledo Yeshiva. In 1491, Rabbeinu Yitzchak Abarbenel studied with him. Rabbeinu Yitzchak Abohav II wrote many works, including a commentary on *Arba'ah Turim* of Rabbeinu Yaakov ben Asher, the son of the R'ash. Although this latest work has been lost, it is quoted extensively in the commentaries of Rabbeinu Yosef Caro, the author of the *Shulchan Aruch*, who refers to him as one of the greatest scholars of his generation. The authorship of *Menoras Hamaor* is sometimes erroneously attributed to the better known Rabbeinu Yitzchak Abohav II, but the Chida proves that this is not so. (See also *Toldos Haposkim* under *"Aron Ha'edus"*.)

Part I:

ROSH HASHANAH

(Chap. 1-5)

Chapter One

PREPARING FOR JUDGMENT

Any intelligent person who is scheduled for trial before a mortal king of flesh and blood will surely spend sleepless days and nights preparing his case. He will seek the advice of every knowledgable person he knows that can help him prepare his case. He will go to great lengths to attain a favorable verdict, even if all that is at stake is but a small part of his fortune and he faces no personal risk. Should he not do so as well when he is brought to judgment before the Supreme King of Kings, the Holy Blessed One? When he himself, his children, and his fortune all hang in the balance?

Indeed, nothing can be concealed from the Holy Blessed One. He needs no witnesses and no evidence; He knows all. And no advocates can plead before Him other than a person's own good deeds and teshuvah for his transgressions. Before such an awesome trial any intelligent person must certainly tremble with fear. He must prepare very thoroughly, examining his actions closely and repenting his sins. As Rosh Hashanah, the Day of Judgment, approaches he must seek any advice he can get that will help him obtain a favorable verdict.

Therefore, it is important to begin preparing for Rosh Hashanah at least thirty days earlier, from Rosh Chodesh of the month of Elul. This is the minimum time required to rouse oneself fully from one's year-long stupor.

Furthermore, the month of Elul is a period of grace during which the Holy Blessed One views the Jewish people as a whole with favor and forgives their sins, for it is the month during which Moshe Rabbeinu went up to Mount Sinai to receive the Second Tablets of the Commandments. The Midrash tells us (Pirkei d'Rabbi Eliezer 46):

It was taught: On Rosh Chodesh of Elul the Holy Blessed One

15

said to Moshe: "Come up to Me to the Mount (Devarim 10:1)."

This was the time when Moshe went up to receive the Second Tablets of the Commandments. The sounds of the shofar were trumpeted throughout the encampment letting the people know that Moshe had gone up to the Mount. Thus the people would not mistakenly turn to idolatry.[1]

And the Holy Blessed One was exalted through the sound of that shofar, as it is written, The Lord ascends amidst the teruah, God amidst the sound of the shofar (Tehillim 47:6).

Therefore, the Sages decreed that each year the shofar be blown from Rosh Chodesh throughout the entire month of Elul. This is to warn the Jewish people to do teshuvah, as it is written, Can a shofar be blown in a city and the people not tremble? (Amos 3:6), and also in order to confuse Satan.[2]

---

1. [Translator's note: This is a reference to the incident of the worshipping of the golden calf-idol. On the seventh day of the month of Sivan, when Moshe Rabbeinu went up to Mount Sinai to receive the First Tablets of the Commandments, he told the Jewish people that he would return after forty days during the first six hours of the day. He returned on the seventeenth day of the month of Tamuz. This calculation of forty days was based on full twenty-four hour periods and did not include the day of his ascendance. The people mistakenly counted that first day as well. According to their calculation Moshe was due to return on the morning of the sixteenth day of Tamuz. When Moshe did not appear on what they considered the fortieth day they were sure that he would never return, and they succumbed to the worship of the golden calf-idol. Therefore, when Moshe went up to receive the Second Tablets of the Commandments the shofar was blown in the encampment every day to warn the people not to err again and turn to idolatry.]

2. [Translator's note: This is a reference to the fact that Satan caused the people to turn to idolatry when Moshe Rabbeinu went up to receive the First Tablets of the Commandments. The Talmud tells us (Shabbos 89a) that on the fortieth day, according to the mistaken calculation of the people (see Footnote 1), Satan appeared and confused the world.

He asked the people: "Where is your master?"

They replied: "He ascended to the Upper World."

He said to them: "The morning of the fortieth day has already passed."

They paid no attention to him.

He said to them: "He has died."

They paid no attention to him.

Then he showed them the image of Moshe's deathbed, and they finally believed him.

Thus, when Moshe went up to receive the second Tablets the shofar was blown to confuse Satan to prevent him from misleading the Jewish people.]

In the responsa of the Geonim we find mention of the various customs pertaining to the month of Elul, including both the blowing of the shofar and the saying of special prayers of entreaty, the Selichos.

Rav Hai Gaon writes: "It is our custom to say Selichos only during the Ten Days of Teshuvah. We have heard, however, that in some places in Persia it is the custom to say these prayers during the entire preceding month of Elul as well, because this is the period during which Moshe went up to Heaven for the third time, returning with the Second Tablets on Yom Kippur. Additional entreaty will certainly bring one only benefit."

Rabbi Yitzchak Ibn Giyas writes: "We follow the custom of beginning from Rosh Chodesh of Elul."

Rabbeinu Nissim writes: "Many elders and householders blow the shofar from Rosh Chodesh of Elul. I have found the source for this custom in the Midrash..." He then goes on to quote the aforementioned passage from Pirkei d'Rabbi Eliezer.

As part of the preparations for the Day of Judgment we also find the custom of fasting on the day before Rosh Hashanah. The basis for this custom can be found in the Midrash (Tanchuma Emor 22):

> It is written, And you shall take for yourselves on the first day the fruit of beautiful trees, branches of palm trees, twigs of myrtle trees, and willows of the brook (Vayikra 23:40).
>
> Why does the verse refer to "the first day'? Doesn't the Festival of Sukkos fall on the fifteenth day of Tishrei?
>
> Only, this refers to the first day of the new accounting of transgression.
>
> There is an analogy to this. One of the king's provinces owed taxes to the king but had not paid. The king mustered an army and set out to the province to collect the overdue taxes. As the king approached within ten parsas[3] of the province the most prominent inhabitants came out to greet him.
>
> They said: "We have nothing, and we cannot pay."

---

3. [Translator's note: A parsah is a Persian mile equivalent to about four miles.]

The king cancelled one third of the debt.

As the king approached even closer to the province the middle level people came out to greet him and plead their cause.

The king cancelled yet another third of the debt.

As the king approached even closer all the inhabitants came out to greet him and plead their cause.

The king cancelled the entire debt.

The king in this analogy represents the Holy Blessed One; the inhabitants of the province are analogous to the Jewish people who transgress all year and accumulate a large debt. On the day before Rosh Hashanah the most prominent among the Jewish people fast, and the Holy Blessed One forgives one third of their guilt. During the Ten Days of Teshuvah the middle level fasts, and the Holy Blessed One forgives another third of the guilt of the Jewish people. On Yom Kippur everyone fasts, and the Holy Blessed One forgives their entire guilt. During the short period of time between Yom Kippur and the Festival of Sukkos people are preoccupied with the mitzvos of sukkah and lulav; they do not have the opportunity to sin. Therefore, the beginning of the Festival of Sukkos is called ''the first day'' of the new accounting of transgression.

It should be noted, however, that those who fast on the day before Rosh Hashanah are nevertheless required to bathe, have their hair cut, and dress in white garments. The Yerushalmi tells us (Rosh Hashanah 1:3):

Rabbi Seemon said: ''It is written, For what great nation is there that has deities close to it, as is God our Lord whenever we call out to Him? (Devarim 4:7).

''Rabbi Chanina and Rabbi Yehoshua explained: 'What other nation can compare to this nation in its familiarity with the laws and customs of its lords? In the way of the world, if a person is scheduled for trial he puts on black garments, wraps himself in a black cloak, lets his beard grow, and does not cut his fingernails, since he does not know what the verdict will be. Not so are the Jewish people. They put on white garments and wrap themselves in white cloaks. They trim their hair and cut their fingernails.

They eat and drink and are joyful on Rosh Hashanah. For they are confident that the Holy Blessed One will perform a miracle for them.' ''

Clearly, Rosh Hashanah is a time for festivity, not fasting. This point is stated explicitly in one of the responsa of the Geonim, which reads as follows:

''As to fasting during the two days of Rosh Hashanah it is our considered opinion that one should not fast. For we find that the early leaders of the Jewish people told them, as the verse quotes, Go eat rich foods and drink sweet drinks, and send portions to those for whom nothing is prepared, for this day is sanctified for our Lord, and be not sad, for the joy of God is your fortress (Nechemiah 8:10). Similarly, we do not approve of fasting on the Shabbos between Rosh Hashanah and Yom Kippur (known as Shabbos Shuvah). For even Tisha b'Av (the Ninth of Av), which is a very important mandatory fast day, is postponed if it falls on Shabbos...

''The Yerushalmi tells us that Rabbi Yaakov used to instruct his scribes to permit fasting on any day but for Shabbos, the Festivals, Rosh Chodesh, and Purim (Nedarim 8:2). The Talmud also mentions that abstention from physical pleasure has no place on Shabbos and the Festivals (Yoma 81a).''

These sources prove the folly of those who fast on Rosh Hashanah and Shabbos Shuvah. Obviously, these people do not realize that teshuvah can be accomplished without fasting. Actually, fasting is only one of the various approaches to teshuvah. There are others that are more fundamental.

Chapter Two

HISTORICAL BACKGROUND

Rosh Hashanah is the day on which all people are judged on worldly matters, both collectively and as individuals. The Talmud tells us (Rosh Hashanah 8b):

> Our rabbis have taught: It is written, For it is a law for Yisrael, a judgment for the Lord of Yaakov (Tehillim 81:5). This comes to teach us that the Court of the Upper World does not convene until the court of the lower world has declared and sanctified the new month.[4]
>
> It was otherwise taught: It is written, For it is a law for Yisrael (Ibid.).
>
> Based on this verse it would seem that only the people of Yisrael are brought to judgment on Rosh Hashanah. How do we know that the gentile nations are also judged on this day?
>
> The verse concludes, A judgment for the Lord of Yaakov (Ibid.).
>
> Why then was it necessary to single out the Jewish people in the first part of the verse? Why was it not sufficient to include them in the generality of the conclusion of the verse?
>
> This comes to teach us that the Jewish people are brought to judgment first, according to the saying of Rav Chisda.
>
> For Rav Chisda said: "If a king and his populace are brought to trial the king is judged first, as it is written, To execute the judgment of His servant and the judgment of His people Yisrael (Melachim I 8:59)."
>
> Why is this so?
>
> It can be said: Because it is improper to have a king sitting and waiting while another is being judged.

---

4. [Translator's note: This derivation is based on the juxtaposition of the verse to the previous verse, Blow the shofar at the new moon, at the time appointed for the day of our festival (Tehillim 81:4).]

It can also be said: Because early judgment is more favorable, since the Divine Wrath has not yet been fully aroused.

Elsewhere, the Talmud also tells us (Rosh Hashanah 16a):

The world is judged four times during the year: On Pesach the harvest is determined. On Shavuos the produce of the trees is determined. On Rosh Hashanah all the inhabitants of the world pass before Him as sheep of the flock, as it is written, He molds their hearts together (Tehillim 33:15). On Sukkos the rainfall is determined.

A closer look at the historical background of Rosh Hashanah, the first day of the month of Tishrei, and all the momentous events that occurred on this date, will give us a better insight into the auspiciousness of this date for the Day of Judgment. The Talmud tells us (Rosh Hashanah 10b):

It was taught: Rabbi Eliezer says: "The world was created during the month of Tishrei. Our forefathers [Avraham and Yaakov] were born during Tishrei. Our forefathers died during Tishrei. Our forefather Yitzchak was born on Pesach. Sarah, Rachel, and Chanah conceived on Rosh Hashanah. Yosef was released from prison on Rosh Hashanah. Our ancestors were freed from their labors in Egypt on Rosh Hashanah, although they were not actually released from Egypt until the month of Nissan. And the ultimate redemption will come during Tishrei."
...And it was also taught: Rabbi Eliezer says: "How do we know that the world was created during Tishrei?
"For it is written, And the Lord said, Let the earth bring forth vegetation, plants yielding seed, and trees bearing fruit... (Beraishis 1:11). During which month does the earth bring forth vegetation and do the trees grow fruit? I would assume that it is Tishrei. Also, that time was a time of rainfall, and the rains came down and made the land bloom, as it is written, And a mist arose from the land and watered the whole face of the earth (Beraishis 2:6), a further indication that the world was created during Tishrei, the rainy season."

And Rabbi Yehoshua says: "How do we know that the world was created during Nissan?

"For it is written, And the earth yielded vegetation... (Beraishis 1:12). During which month is the earth already full of vegetation and are the trees already full of fruit? I would assume that it is Nissan. Also, that time was a time of animal mating, as it is written, The pastures were clothed with sheep (Tehillim 65:14), a further indication that the world was created during Nissan."

...Rabbi Eliezer says: "How do we know that our forefathers were born during Tishrei?

"For it is written, And all the men of Yisrael gathered around the king, Shlomo, during the Month of the Mighty on the festival... (Melachim I 8:2). The reference to Tishrei as 'the Month of the Mighty' indicates that the Mighty Ancients were born during this month."

...And Rabbi Yehoshua says: "How do we know that our forefathers were born during Nissan?

"For it is written, And it was in the four hundred and eightieth year after the people of Yisrael went forth from the land of Mitzraim, in the fourth year, in the Month of Brilliance... (Melachim I 6:1). This reference to Nissan as 'the Month of Brilliance' indicates that the Brilliant Ancients were born during this month."

...The one who says our forefathers were born during Tishrei also says that they died during Tishrei. The one who says our forefathers were born during Nissan also says that they died during Nissan. How do they know this?

Because it is written, And he said to them, I am one hundred and twenty years old today (Devarim 31:2).

What is the significance of "today'?

Moshe was telling the Jewish people that on that very day the one hundred and twenty years were completed.

This comes to teach us that the Holy Blessed One figures the years of the life spans of righteous people to the precise day and month, as it is written, And I will make full the number of your days (Shemos 23:26).

...Sarah, Rachel, and Chanah conceived on Rosh Hashanah. How do we know this?

Rabbi Elazar said: "This is derived from the parallel expressions of two different Hebrew words meaning remembering. It is written of Rachel, And the Lord remembered Rachel (Beraishis 30:22), and it is written of Chanah, And God remembered her (Shmuel I 1:19). We find the same Hebrew word used in reference to Rosh Hashanah in that which is written, A remembrance of teruah (Vayikra 23:24). Having established that Chanah conceived on Rosh Hashanah, we can now determine when Sarah conceived. The same Hebrew word is used in that which is written of Chanah, For God remembered Chanah (Shmuel I 2:21), and in that which is written of Sarah, And God remembered Sarah (Beraishis 21:1). This indicates that Chanah and Sarah conceived at the same time of year."

Yosef was released from prison on Rosh Hashanah. How do we know this?

For it is written, Blow the shofar on the new moon...for it is a law for Yisrael...as a testament to Yosef did he establish it when he went out to the land of Mitzraim (Tehillim 81:4-6).

Our fathers were freed from their labors in Egypt on Rosh Hashanah. How do we know this?

It is derived from the parallel expression of the Hebrew word for burden in that which is written, From under the burdens of Mitzraim (Shemos 6:6) and in that which is written of Yosef, I removed his shoulder from the burden (Tehillim 81:17).

They were redeemed from Egypt during Nissan but the ultimate redemption will come during Tishrei. This is derived from the mention of the shofar in reference to Rosh Hashanah in that which is written, Blow the shofar on the new moon (Tehillim 81:4) and in reference to the ultimate redemption in that which is written, And it shall be on that day that a great shofar shall be blown... (Yeshayahu 27:13).

Considering that man was created during Tishrei it is fitting that the new year for all the world's inhabitants should begin at that time. Also, considering that Sarah, Rachel, and Chanah, who were all barren, were "remembered by Hashem" and conceived during Tishrei it is apparently an auspicious time for remembrance. Therefore, it is fitting that the supplications for a healthy and prosperous new year come during this time.

Furthermore, Adam was created on Rosh Hashanah, and on that very same day he sinned, did teshuvah, and was forgiven. And the Holy Blessed One said to him: "Just as I have forgiven you on this day, so too will I forgive the sins of your descendants on this day." Thus, the proper day for judgment, teshuvah, and forgiveness is Rosh Hashanah.

The Pesikta tells us (Piska 23):

> It is written, Forever, O God, is Your Word established in the heavens (Tehillim 119:89), and it is also written, Before Your judgment do they stand on this day (Tehillim 119:91), the inference being that this day had been established as a day of judgment from the beginning of creation.
>
> Rabbi Eliezer says: "The world was created on the twenty-fifth day of Elul."
>
> This explanation is based on that which we have been taught: During the prayers of Rosh Hashanah we say: "This day marks the beginning of Your Deeds." Meaning: On Rosh Hashanah Adam, the primal man, was created. During the first hour of the day, He conceived the plan of creating a man. During the second hour, He sought the counsel of the angels of service. During the third hour, He collected the dust from which He would make the man. During the fourth hour, He kneaded it. During the fifth hour, He shaped it. During the sixth hour, He completed its form. During the seventh hour, He put a soul into it. During the eighth hour, He led the man into the Garden of Eden. During the ninth hour, the man was commanded not to eat from the Tree of Knowledge. During the tenth hour, he transgressed that command. During the eleventh hour, he was judged. During the twelfth hour, he was granted amnesty.
>
> The Holy Blessed One said to Adam: "Just as you stood before Me today and were granted amnesty, so too, in the future, will your descendants stand before Me to be judged on this day and be granted amnesty."

It should be noted, however, that although Rosh Hashanah is the day of judgment certain matters remain pending. They are decided at various appointed times throughout the year. These are times when specific sacrifices were brought in the Bais Hamikdash to seek favor before Him as regards these matters. The Talmud tells us (Rosh Hashanah 16a):

> It was taught: Everything is judged on Rosh Hashanah, but the final verdicts are delivered on each matter in its own time: the grain harvest on Pesach, the harvest of the fruit trees on Atzeres (Shavuos), the rainfall on Sukkos. People are judged on Rosh Hashanah, and their verdicts are sealed on Yom Kippur.
>
> Rabbi Yosi says: "People are judged every single day, as it is written, And You remembered him every morning (Iyov 7:18)."
>
> Rabbi Nassan says: "People are judged at all times, as it is written, You tested him every moment (Ibid.)."
>
> ...It was taught: Rabbi Yehudah says in the name of Rabbi Akiva: "Why did the Torah direct that the omer offering from the new harvest be brought on Pesach?
>
> "Because Pesach comes during harvest time. The Holy Blessed One said: 'Bring Me the omer on Pesach so that the harvest in the fields should be plentiful.'
>
> "Why did the Torah direct that the offering of the two loaves be brought on Atzeres?
>
> "Because Atzeres comes during the harvest from fruit trees. The Holy Blessed One said: 'Bring Me the two loaves on Atzeres so that the harvest from the fruit trees should be plentiful.'
>
> "And why did the Torah direct that the water ablutions be poured in the Bais Hamikdash on Sukkos?
>
> "Because Sukkos comes during the beginning of the rainy season. The Holy Blessed One said: 'Pour the water ablutions before Me on Sukkos so that the year's rainfall should be plentiful.'
>
> "And the Holy Blessed One said: 'Say before Me on Rosh Hashanah the prayers of kingship, remembrance, and the blowing of the shofar. Kingship, to accept Me as your king. Remembrance, so that your remembrance will come favorably before Me. And through what medium? Through the shofar.'"
>
> Rabbi Abahu said: "Why do we blow on Rosh Hashanah with a shofar made from a ram's horn?
>
> "And the Holy Blessed One said: 'Blow before Me on Rosh

*Hashanah with a shofar made from a ram's horn so that I will
recall to your benefit the Akeidah upon which Yitzchak the son of
Avraham was offered up as a sacrifice to Me and replaced by a ram.
Thus will I consider it as if you too have offered yourselves up to
Me as a sacrifice.'"*

Indeed, the Akeidah of Yitzchak is of major significance to the
descendants of our forefather Avraham. Avraham's willingness to
sacrifice his son Yitzchak to fulfill the Will of the Creator earned
him and his offspring the Creator's everlasting love. His conduct
during this ordeal is a source of merit upon which the Jewish people repeatedly draw in perilous times. The Talmud tells us
(Sanhedrin 89b):

*It is written, And it was after these things, and the Lord tested
Avraham (Beraishis 22:1).*

After which things?

*Rabbi Yochanan said in the name of Rabbi Yosi the son of
Zimra: "After the events involving Satan. For it is written, and
the boy grew up, and he was weaned... (Beraishis 21:8).*

*"Satan said to the Holy Blessed One:Master of the Universe,
You have granted this old man a child at the age of one hundred.
Yet, of all the feasts he has made he did not sacrifice before You
even one turtledove or one fledgling.'*

*"He replied:He made these feasts only in honor of the birth of
his son. If I were to tell him to sacrifice that son to Me, he would
do so.'*

*"Thereupon, And the Lord tested Avraham... (Beraishis
22:1)."*

*It is written, And He said, Please take your son, your only one,
that you love, Yitzchak, and go you to the land of Moriah, and offer him up there as a burnt offering on one of the hills that I will
tell you (Beraishis 22:2).*

*Rabbi Shimeon the son of Aba said: "The verse uses terms of
entreaty rather than command. There is an analogy to this. A
mortal king of flesh and blood was beset by many wars. He had one
mighty warrior who fought these wars for him and won them all.*

After a time, the threat of a major war loomed.

"The king said to the warrior:I beg you to wage this war for me so that it not be said that your earlier service was meaningless.'

"So to did the Holy Blessed One say to Avraham:I have put you through many ordeals and you have withstood them all. Now I ask you to withstand this ordeal so that it not be said that the earlier ones were meaningless.' "

The Holy Blessed One said: "Please take your son... (Ibid.)."

Avraham replied: "I have two sons.'5

He continued: "Your only one... (Ibid.)."

Avraham replied: "Each of my sons is his mother's only one."

He continued: "That you love... (Ibid.)."

Avraham replied: "I love both of them."

He continued: "Yitzchak (Ibid.)."

Why was all this necessary? Why didn't He specify Yitzchak directly?

To lessen the shock to Avraham and to protect his sanity.6

Satan went forth to meet Avraham along the way and said to him: "If we try to speak to you will you be wearied? but who can hold back words? behold, you have chastised many, and you have strengthened weak hands, your words have kept erect those that stumbled, and you have supported those with sinking knees, yet now it comes upon you and you are wearied, it touches you and you are confounded (Iyov 4:2-5).'7

Avraham replied: "But I will walk in my innocence (Tehillim 26:11)."

---

5. [Translator's note: Yitzchak the son of Sarah and Yishmael the son of Hagar.]

6. [Translator's note: At first glance, the Talmud seems to be saying that if it had been Yishmael·who was to have been sacrificed it would not have been quite so shocking to Avraham. This is indeed true since Avraham's lineage would be continued through Yitzchak, as it is written, For through Yitzchak shall your offspring be known (Beraishis 21:12). However, It can also be said that as long as the exact nature of the ordeal was not clearly defined its full import did not strike home. Therefore, by being deliberately ambiguous Hashem was gradually preparing Avraham for the shock.]

7. [Translator's note: Rashi explains that Satan was in effect saying: "Can it be that the One who loves you would test you with something that is so troubling to you and will cut off your lineage?']

Satan continued: "Is not your fear folly? (Iyov 4:6)."

Avraham replied: "Remember please whoever perished being innocent (Iyov 4:7)."

When Satan saw that Avraham would not heed him he said: "But to me a word came by stealth (Iyov 4:12). This have I heard from behind the heavenly curtain:A sheep will be the burnt offering; Yitzchak will not be the burnt offering.' "

Avraham replied: "It is the punishment of a liar that even if he tells the truth he is paid no attention."

Rav Levi said "The reference in the verse toafter these things' is to a conversation between Yishmael and Yitzchak.

"Yishmael said to Yitzchak:I am greater than you in the performance of the mitzvos, for you were circumcized when you were eight days old, while I was circumcized at thirteen years of age.'

"Yitzchak replied:Do you pride yourself over me because of just one organ? If the Holy Blessed One would tell me to sacrifice myself before Him I would do so.'

"Thereupon, And the Lord tested Avraham... (Beraishis 22:1)."

As a reminder of Avraham's readiness to sacrifice his son Yitzchak on the Akeidah to fulfill His Will, a ram being substituted at the last moment, Hashem commanded that the shofar, a ram's horn, be blown on Rosh Hashanah.

The verses we read on Rosh Hashanah and the blowing of the shofar are all expressions of teshuvah and our acceptance of His Kingship over us. We read the portion of how He remembered Sarah when she was barren (Beraishis 21) and the Akeidah of Yitzchak (Beraishis 22). And we conclude with the Haftorah reading of how He remembered Chanah when she was barren (Shmuel I 1) and of repentance (Yirmiyahu 31). We implore Him to accept our teshuvah, even if we have not repented perfectly, and to let us benefit from the merit of these righteous women whom He remembered and the Akeidah of Yitzchak. We implore Him to let our remembrance come favorably before Him and to have mercy on us.

Chapter Three

REWARD AND RETRIBUTION

All the principles of the Torah and our beliefs are based on the concept of total and universal Divine Providence, the belief that the Creator controls and guides every aspect of the world, both in the general sense and the individual sense, dealing with each person according to his deeds.[8] There are countless references to this concept in the Torah. Our Sages have told us (Avos 3:15):

Everything is observed by Hashem, and choice is granted to people; the world is judged through His goodness, but everything is determined according to the preponderance of deeds.

Although it is certainly true that He is constantly guiding the world, giving out reward and punishment as each situation warrants, on Rosh Hashanah there is a general accounting. It is a time when a person's every deed is placed on the scale of justice to determine if it will be tipped to his favor or detriment.[9] Nothing is forgotten when a person is brought to judgment before the Throne of Glory. In fact, in order that the common people understand perfectly, our Sages speak in the allegory of deeds being recorded in the Book of Remembrance to underscore the fact that He remembers everything. The Talmud tells us (Rosh Hashanah 16b):

Rabbi Kruspidai said in the name of Rabbi Yochanan: "Three separate books are opened on Rosh Hashanah. One contains the records of the absolutely righteous, another contains the records

---

8. As it is written, Great in counsel and mighty in exploits, that Your Eyes are vigilant over all the ways of people, to give each man according to his ways, according to the fruits of his actions (Yirmiyahu 32:19). And it is written, The Eyes of God, they examine the entire earth (Zechariah 4:10).

9. As symbolized by the sign of the month of Tishrei which is Libra, or scales.

of the absolutely sinful, and a third contains the records of average people. The book of the absolutely righteous is immediately inscribed with the verdict of life and sealed. The book of the absolutely sinful is immediately inscribed with the verdict of death and sealed. The book of average people is left pending from Rosh Hashanah until Yom Kippur. If they are found worthy the verdict of life is inscribed. If they are found unworthy the verdict of death is inscribed.''

Rabbi Avin said: ''From where is this derived? From that which is written, They shall be erased from the book of life, and they shall not be inscribed with the righteous (Tehillim 69:29).

'' 'They shall be erased from the book' is an allusion to the absolutely sinful.

'' 'Life' is an allusion to the absolutely righteous.

'' 'And they shall not be inscribed with the righteous' is an allusion to average people.''

Rav Nachman the son of Yitzchak said: ''The allusion can be found in that which is written, But if not, please erase me from Your Book which You have written (Shemos 32:32).

'' 'Please erase me' is an allusion to the absolutely sinful.

'' 'From Your Book' is an allusion to the absolutely righteous.

'' 'Which You have written' is an allusion to average people.''

It was taught: The disciples of the school of Shamai say: ''On the day of judgment the judged are divided into three groups: One consists of the thoroughly righteous; one consists of the thoroughly sinful; one consists of average people.

''For the group of the thoroughly righteous, it is immediately inscribed and sealed that they are to live in the world to come...''

Many scholars have commented on the perplexing nature of this passage from the Talmud, pointing out that we sometimes find that a righteous man perishes in spite of his righteousness, while a sinful man endures in spite of his sinfulness.[10] Indeed, we find that this perplexity troubled even David Hamelech, who wrote, And I nearly set out... for I was jealous of the wanton, when I saw the tranquility of the sinful (Tehillim 73:1-2). This

---

10. [Translator's note: A reference to Koheles 7:15.]

observation did not let him rest, until he concluded, Not until I come to the Sanctum of the Lord will I perceive their ultimate fate (Tehillim 73:17). His intention can be interpreted either as their "ultimate fate" immediately after their death or as their "ultimate fate" in the world to come. The prophet Yirmiyahu also expressed a similar perplexity, Why is the way of the sinful prosperous? (Yirmiyahu 12:1).

It would appear that their perplexity was focused more on the success of the sinful rather than on the suffering of the righteous. This is because there is no righteous man in the world who does only good and never sins.[11] Thus, someone who might appear to be a righteous person might actually be guilty of secret sins. Those people, however, who are openly sinful and still enjoy peace and tranquility are certainly a cause for great perplexity.

Our Sages have anticipated these questions (Taanis 11a).[12] They quote that which is written, The Lord of Trust with no injustice (Devarim 32:4), pointing out that He has no prejudice or partiality. It is possible that someone who is steeped in sinfulness might nevertheless have done something meritorious. Therefore, He rewards that sinful person thoroughly in this world so that he will have no claim to reward in the world to come. Similarly, it is possible that a righteous person might have been guilty of some sin. Therefore, He exacts full retribution from him in this world so that he may be thoroughly rewarded in the world to come.

Consequently, if we see an apparently righteous person die before his time, or someone sinful live long, it is because the judgment of Rosh Hashanah does not determine the fate of the soul but the fate of the body. Rabbi Yochanan was saying that only those who are absolutely righteous, completely free of guilt, are immediately inscribed for life in this world, and that only those who are absolutely sinful, completely lacking in merit, are immediately inscribed for death. The judgment to determine the fate of the soul in the world to come comes only after death. This judgment is discussed in the conclusion of the above passage from the Talmud

---

11. [Translator's note: A reference to Koheles 7:20.]

12. [Translator's note: For full text and discussion see Prologue to the First Light of the Menorah, *The Light of Contentment.*]

in the name of the disciples of the school of Shamai (not quoted here).

Others offer a different explanation for the incidence of misfortune among some righteous people.[13] They contend that if the Creator were to grant prosperity, tranquility, and long life in this world to the righteous, while denying these benefits to and even visiting immediate retribution upon the sinful, the purpose of the Torah would be defeated. All people would then automatically decide to be righteous. Their primary motivation, however, would be mere practicality. They would neither be doing it for the sake of Heaven, nor for the deep significance of the acts, nor to achieve the glorious ultimate rewards outlined in the Torah. They would be doing it only to achieve immediate material benefits and to avoid immediate retribution. Therefore, the Creator has designed the world in such a way that material reward and retribution are not always in direct proportion to righteousness and sinfulness. Only thus will people serve Him expressly for the sake of fulfilling His Will and achieving spiritual reward. Only thus will immediate material benefit and the avoidance of retribution be relegated to secondary motivations for their righteousness.

Indeed, people cannot be expected to react otherwise. It is in the very nature of the species to instinctively seek that which is beneficial and to recoil from that which is harmful. All living creatures react this way purely out of instinct. If a hungry beast finds grass or a thirsty beast finds water it will immediately try to satisfy its need, but it will be very careful to avoid ditches or thorns that stand in its way. Certainly, people who are endowed with the ability to make logical choices will choose what benefits them and avoid what harms them. Even a small child who is presented with a smoldering coal and a pearl will always choose the pearl.

In fact, even now that the relationship between righteousness and reward is not perfectly clear, our Sages have found it necessary to tell us not to serve the Blessed Lord in order to be

---

13. [Translator's note: Elsewhere, the author cites *Sha'ar Hashamayim* by Rabbi Yitzchak ben Letef as the source for this opinion. See Epilogue to the Third Light of the Menorah, *The Light of Mitzvos*.]

rewarded but for the sake of Heaven (Avos 1:3). Service should be for the realization of truth; honors will come ultimately. If the relationship between righteousness and reward *were* perfectly clear people would inevitably be improperly motivated.

Furthermore, if all righteous people would experience only good and all sinful people misfortune the balance of nature would be disrupted. No longer would the natural order of events be determined by positive and negative factors within nature itself. It would then be quite possible that a pious person would habitually eat unwholesome foods without experiencing discomfort or illness. He might even throw himself off a high place and escape harm. Conversely, a sinful person might sow a fertile field and nothing would grow, even if his field is right next to the field of a pious person which is in full bloom. It might even rain on the field of the pious person but not on the field of the sinful person. Also, the sinful person might marry and not have children. Such eventualities are a negation of the natural order which the Creator instilled in the world. Nature must be permitted to run its course, at least in outward appearance.[14]

Therefore, we must be content not to focus so intently on material benefit in this world. Such rewards are empty compared to the peaceful bliss of the world to come. Even if the righteous person falters in this world he will surely be successful in the world to come. And even if the sinful person is successful in this world he will surely have his downfall in the world to come. We must keep in mind that all reward is limited and temporary except for the peace and security of the eternal world to come, as the prophet has written, No eye has seen a deity beside you, who provides for the one that waits for Him (Yeshayahu 64:3).

In summation, we find that although teshuvah and good deeds are always effective, they are of particular importance as we approach the day of judgment. At this time, when one's self, one's

---

14. [Translator's note: This does not mean that righteous people are not rewarded with good in this world. It merely means that there must not be an incontrovertible cause and effect relationship between righteousness and material reward. Manipulation of natural forces and circumstances to benefit the righteous person does not subvert the natural process. Only inevitability subverts the natural process.]

children, and one's livelihood are judged a person must be especially careful to remove his sins through teshuvah. Thus can he be assured of a favorable verdict and of being immediately inscribed for life. Even if he will only attain the level of an average person whose merits and demerits are in balance, his scale will be tipped to his favor and he will merit being inscribed for life after Yom Kippur.[15] The abovementioned passage from the Talmud which tells us that if average people are found unworthy on Yom Kippur the verdict of death is inscribed refers only to those who fail to do teshuvah.[16]

The Talmud tells us that the best time for the individual to do teshuvah is during the days between Rosh Hashanah and Yom Kippur (Rosh Hashana 18a). This is the time when He is most willing to accept teshuvah, the time of which the prophet says, Entreat God when He can be found, call out to Him when He is near (Yeshayahu 55:6),[17] the time referred to in that which is written, And from there you shall seek out God your Lord, and you shall find Him if you entreat with all your heart and all your soul (Devarim 4:29).

---

15. [Translator's note: This is according to the opinion of the disciples of the school of Hillel. For full text and discussion see the First Light of the Menorah, *The Light of Contentment*, Section I, Chapter 8.]

16. This is because it is incumbent on each person to do teshuvah, as it is written, And you shall return to God your Lord, and you shall listen to His Voice (Devarim 4:31). The transgression of this mitzvah tips the otherwise balanced scale of average people to their detriment.

17. [Translator's note: According to the interpretation of this verse in Pesikta (Piska 24).]

Chapter Four

THE SHOFAR'S CALL TO TESHUVA

Because of His mercy for his creatures the Blessed Lord has given them the opportunity to do teshuvah and be spared the consequences of their misdeeds. He knows that the inborn inclination of people is to sin[18] and that by nature they gravitate towards the material rather than the intellectual. Therefore, He has required people to examine their ways constantly and to return through teshuvah.[19]

In actuality, however, people are caught up in their material drives throughout the year and are not constantly inspired to do teshuvah. For this reason, the Torah has directed that the shofar be blown on Rosh Hashanah to urge and remind them to do teshuvah. The blowing of the shofar is, in effect, saying: "Rouse yourselves from your slumber, you sleeping ones, for the time of your judgment approaches. The blessed Lord, who seeks not the destruction of the sinful but their return through teshuvah, has called out to the Jewish people through the blowing of the shofar on Rosh Hashanah and exhorted them to do teshuvah." Then, if the shofar is blown in the city and the people do not tremble[20] their blood is on their own hands.

The Pesikta tells us (Piska 25):

> It is written, And God calls out before His army, for his encampment is very numerous, for powerful is the one who fulfills His Word, for great is the day of God, and very awesome, and who can withstand it? (Yoel 2:11).
> "And God calls out" on Rosh Hashanah. "For his encamp-

---

18. [Translator's note: A reference to Beraishis 8:21.]
19. As it is written, Let us examine our ways and investigate, and let us return to God (Eichah 3:40).
20. [Translator's note: A reference to Amos 3:6.]

*ment is very numerous" refers to the Jewish people. "For power-
ful is the one who fulfills His word" means that He enhances the
power of the righteous people who fulfill His Will. "For great is
the day of God, and very awesome" refers to Yom Kippur.*

*"And who can withstand it" is explained by that which Rabbi
Kruspidai said in the name of Rabbi Yochanan: "There are three
accounts: one for the thoroughly righteous, one for the
thoroughly sinful, and one for average people.*

*" 'Those for eternal life'[21] refers to the thoroughly righteous.
'And these for disgrace and everlasting shame' refers to the
thoroughly sinful.*

*" 'They shall be erased from the book'[22] refers to the thoroughly
sinful. 'Life' refers to the thoroughly righteous. 'And they shall
not be inscribed with the righteous' refers to average people. The
Holy Blessed One has granted the average people the ten days between Rosh Hashanah and Yom Kippur as a grace period. If they
do teshuvah they are inscribed with the righteous; if not they are
inscribed with the sinful.*

Since the purpose of the blowing of the shofar is to arouse the
people to do teshuvah, the Torah has directed that it be blown in
the sequence of tekiah, teruah, tekiah. These sounds correspond
to the three elements of teshuvah. The tekiah sound is a long
trumpet blast. It is blown first to symbolize that the person doing
teshuvah must look into and closely examine his ways. He must
break completely with his sinful ways. If he has any guilt, even in
his heart or mind, he must purge it.[23]

The teruah sound is a tremulous wailing sound. It is blown second to symbolize the second stage of teshuvah, that the person
doing teshuvah must lament and wail over his transgressions, that
he must regret the sinfulness of his deeds.[24]

---

21. [Translator's note: Rabbi Yochanan is referring to Daniel 12:2.]

22. [Translator's note: Rabbi Yochanan is referring to Tehillim 69:29.]

23. As it is written, Let the villain abandon his ways, and the guilty man his
thoughts, and let him return (Yeshayahu 55:7).

24. As it is written, After I returned I was regretful, and after I was made aware
I beat upon my thigh, I was embarrassed, and also ashamed, for I bore the
disgrace of my youth (Yirmiyahu 31:18).

Finally, the tekiah is blown again to symbolize the final stage of teshuvah, the deep resolve never to return to the sinful attitudes and deeds.[25]

The Torah refers to these three stages of teshuvah when it describes the ease of doing teshuvah in that which is written, For this mitzvah that I command you today is not difficult for you, nor is it far off, it is not in the heavens, that you can say, Who will go up for us to the heavens and take it for us, and impart it, that we may do it? and it is not across the sea, that you can say, Who will cross over for us to the other side of the sea and take it for us, and impart it to us, that we may do it? for this thing is very near to you, in your mouth, and in your heart, to do it (Devarim 30:11-14).

The Torah is telling us that the teshuvah which it directs the Jewish people to do is more accessible and easier than that required of other peoples by their own religions.

Members of other religions who transgress and seek the advice of their priests as to repentance are advised to subject themselves to the most severe penance to expurgate their sins. They are told to fast for many days and to trudge to distant lands, barefoot, weary, and exhausted. They are told to flagellate themselves with metal rods and to undergo other horrible tortures.

The holy Torah, however, is solicitous of the welfare of the Jewish people. It does not demand many fasts or great torture or long journeys. It does not demand that one scale impossible peaks or travel to distant lands across the sea. "it is not in the heavens . . . and it is not across the sea," the Torah tells us. "For this thing is very near to you, in your mouth, and in your heart, to do it.

These last three phrases refer to the three stages of teshuvah, which are represented by the mouth, the heart, and deeds. At first, the mouth must acknowledge the transgressions and declare that they are being abandoned. Then the person doing teshuvah must lament and be heartbroken over his transgressions. Finally, the sincerity of his teshuvah must be manifest in his deeds, never

---

25. As it is written, And we will no longer say that the works of our hands are deities, for it is in You that the orphan finds mercy (Hoshaya 14:4).

reverting to his earlier transgressions.[26]

Our Sages have also directed that the shofar be blown once again during the *Mussaf* prayers. The Talmud tells us that the purpose of this is to confuse Satan[27] (Rosh Hashanah 16a). There is a further Midrashic explanation. It states that the first blowing of the shofar arouses the fear of those who hear it. And when they hear it again their fear becomes heightened and more effective.

It would also appear to me that the blowing of the shofar confuses Satan by reminding him of his ultimate fate. When he hears the shofar he is reminded that in the end of days when the great shofar is blown to announce the final redemption[28] he will be destroyed for eternity.[29] Just as a human prosecutor who is reminded of his impending death becomes disoriented and unable to prosecute effectively, so too is it with Satan.

We also find in the Responsa of Rabbi Yitzchak Ibn Giyas (Responsa 175 and 176) that Rav Amram, Rabbeinu Saadya, and Rabbeinu Hai would customarily blow the shofar a third time, after the conclusion of the prayers, in order to further confuse Satan.

It is interesting to note that the Torah refers to Rosh Hashanah as "the Day of Teruah,"[30] rather than as "the Day of Tekiah". This is because one who is truly regretful of his sins wails and laments over them. Thus, it is the middle stage, symbolized by the teruah, which is most important, because it indicates that one has truly abandoned one's sinful ways and will not readily return to them. Also, the word "teruah" is an expression of brokenheartedness, as it written, You shall break them with an iron rod (Tehillim 2:9).

The poet has written of the importance of understanding the

---

26. These verses can also be interpreted as referring to the Torah rather than to teshuvah. According to this interpretation the explanation is as follows: All the mitzvos of the Torah, both positive commandments and prohibitions, must be performed on three levels—verbal expression, inner consciousness, and overt deeds.

27. [Translator's note: See Chapter 1.]

28. [Translator's note: According to Yeshayahu 27:13.]

29. As it is written, And death will be consumed forever (Yeshayahu 27:8), Satan being synonymous with death.

30. Bamidbar 29:1.

meaning of the teruah, saying, Fortunate are the people that know the teruah (Tehillim 89:16). And he concludes. O God, they shall walk in the radiance of Your Face (Ibid). Hashem will shine the radiance of His Face upon the people who do teshuvah, and He will draw them close to His great Name with love.

Chapter Five

THE TEN SYMBOLS OF TESHUVA

All of the mitzvos have many properties that are beneficial both to the body and the soul. Therefore, when the Holy Blessed One wanted to increase the merit of the Jewish people, whom He had chosen above all the peoples, He gave them many laws of the Torah and mitzvos from which they would gain advantage. The mitzvah of blowing the shofar on Rosh Hashanah as well has many purposes, and all of them pave the upward path for the intelligent.[31] They fall into the following categories:

1. On this day man was created. This was the culmination of the creation of the lower world which was designed as a setting for people. Thus, Rosh Hashanah signifies the day during which the Holy Blessed One assumed the kingship of the creatures of the world. It is a well-known custom on the anniversary of the ascendance to the throne of a mortal king of flesh and blood for his servants to gather and to blow trumpets in honor of the occasion, as if to proclaim: "Long live our master, the King!" The Supreme King of Kings, the Holy Blessed One, whose kingship preceded his nation, whose kingship is eternal and uninterrupted is certainly worthy of the same honor. And so the poet writes, With trumpets and the sound of the shofar blow before the King, God (Tehillim 98:6).

2. This is the period designated for the acceptance of those returning. The Torah, therefore, directed that the shofar be blown to announce that whoever wishes to return should do so now, and whoever doesn't has his own blood on his hands. What better warning could there be? It is the practice of kings to publicize their decrees so that the people should abide by them and that whoever doesn't will bear guilt. And it is also the practice of kings who wish to grant amnesty to make a proclamation saying: "Whoever comes forward during the designated period of time and resumes the ser-

---

31. [Translator's note: A reference to Mishlei 15:24.]

40

vice of the king will be forgiven; whoever doesn't has only himself to blame.'' So too is the significance of the blowing of the shofar.

3. The blowing of the shofar reminds us of the gathering at Mount Sinai to receive the Torah, because at that time too was the shofar blown, as it is written, And the sound of the shofar grew very strong (Shemos 19:19). The memory of that awesome spectacle induces fear of the Holy Blessed One in our hearts, and we resolve to perform the mitzvos in the manner He prescribed and to do teshuvah for our transgressions.

4. The blowing of the shofar reminds us of the words of the prophets, which are compared to the sound of the shofar, as it is written, And whoever hears the sound of the shofar and is not heedful, the sword shall come and take him, his blood shall be on his own head (Yechezkel 33:4). When we remember their admonitions, and take heed of them, we ensure safety for our households and all we possess.

5. The blowing of the shofar reminds us of the destruction of the Bais Hamikdash, which was to the accompaniment of the battle trumpets of the enemy, as it is written, For my soul heard the sound of the shofar, the trumpet call of war (Yirmiyahu 4:19).

6. The blowing of the shofar reminds us of the Akeidah upon which our forefather Yitzchak was willing to give up his life for the glory of his Master to fulfill His Will. And it reminds us of his father Avraham who loved him no less than himself, yet was willing to sacrifice him to heed the Words of Hashem. But the Holy Blessed One took mercy on the father and the son. He showed them the ram that was created at the same time as Adam, and he accepted it as a burnt offering instead of Yitzchak, considering it as if Avraham had indeed sacrificed his son as a perfect burnt offering. If we follow in his footsteps the Creator will have mercy on us as well and remember his righteousness to our credit as the Talmud tells us (Rosh Hashanah 16a):

The Holy Blessed One said: ''Blow before Me on the shofar of a ram so that I will remember to your credit the Akeidah of Yitzchak the son of Avraham. I will accept your teshuvah, and I will rescue you from your enemies and adversaries.''

7. The blowing of the shofar awakens fear and terror in us. Such is the instinctive reaction to this sound. Thus will we humble ourselves before our Creator, as it is written, Can a shofar be blown in the city and the people not tremble? (Amos 3:6). People hearing the sound of the shofar will ask each other: "What is significant about today?" And they will be told the reasons. The Rambam writes (Teshuvah 3:4):'Although the blowing of the shofar is an unexplained Scriptural decree its meaning is suggested. It is as if to say: 'Sleeping ones! Rouse yourselves from your slumber and examine your deeds. Remember your Creator and return through teshuvah. Do not be among those who are oblivious to the truth, preoccupied by the foolishness of the moment, who spend all their lives caught up in foolishness and emptiness that provide no benefit or protection. Look at yourselves! Look at your actions and your deeds! Let each one of you abandon his sinful ways and attitudes which bear no good. Let him return to God, and He will have mercy on him.' "[32]

8. The blowing of the shofar reminds us of the great day of judgment that comes after death, and thus, it arouses fear in us. For it is written, The great day of God draws near, it draws near very quickly, the sound of the day of God, the mighty man cries bitterly there, that day is a day of wrath, a day of anguish and distress, a day of waste and desolation, a day of darkness and gloom, a day of clouds and fog, a day of the shofar and teruah against the fortified cities and the high battlements (Zephaniah 1:16). And the prophet continues, Gather yourselves together and assemble, O nation without longing (Zephaniah 2:1).

9. The blowing of the shofar signifies that the Holy Blessed One will gather in the banished of Yisrael, as promised by the prophet Yeshayahu, And it shall be on that day a great shofar will be blown... (Yeshayahu 27:13).

10. The blowing of the shofar reminds us of the resurrection of the dead. The prophet has described that day, saying that a shofar will be blown, and they will all gather at the sound of it, as it is written, All the inhabitants of the world and those who dwell in

---

32. [Translator's note: A reference to Yeshayahu 55:7.]

the earth, when the banner is lifted upon the mountain you shall see and when the shofar is blown you shall hear (Yeshayahu 18:3). "The inhabitants of the world" refers to the Jews in the Diaspora. "Those who dwell in the earth" refers to the dead, as we find a similar usage in that which is written, Your dead shall be revived, my dead cadavers shall arise, wake up and sing, dwellers in the dust... (Yeshayahu 26:19).

It is therefore important that we familiarize ourselves with all of the various meanings of the blowing of the shofar.[33] It is clear, however. that the underlying theme of Rosh Hashanah is the call to do teshuvah and abandon our sinful ways. (The liturgy of Rosh Hashanah is discussed in *The Light of Mitzvos*, Section III, Chapter 25, and spelled out in greater detail in *Shulchan Hapanim*.[34]) The Midrash tells us (Vayikra Rabah 29:6):

> *The Holy Blessed One said to the people of Yisrael:'If you will beautify your deeds before Me I will be as a shofar[35] for you. Just as the shofar takes in breath from one side and releases it on the other, so too will I arise from the Throne of Strict Judgment and sit on the throne of Merciful Judgment. I will have mercy on you.''*

---

33. Careful observance of the mitzvos is to our benefit, as it is written, And God commanded us to execute all these laws, to fear God our Lord, that it might benefit us for all the days... (Devarim 6:24).

34. [Translator's note: *Shulchan Hapanim* is a halachic work written by the author. It is part of a trilogy that also includes *Menoras Hamaor* and *Aron Ha'edus*, one of the earliest codifications of the Halacha. *Shulchan Hapanim*, actually a subdivision of *Aron Ha'edus*, deals with berachos (blessings) and tefillos (prayers). The only work of this trilogy extant is *Menoras Hamaor*. (See the First Light of the Menorah, *The Light of Contentment*, Translator's Foreword and Appendix A: Ode to the Menorah.)]

35. [Translator's note: The roots of the Hebrew word shofar and the Hebrew word used here for beautify are identical.] *

Part II:

YOM KIPPUR

(Chap. 6-8)

Chapter Six

PREPARING FOR ATONEMENT

Any intelligent person who fears the Word of God should tremble inwardly when he realizes that all his deeds are recorded and that the Lord will incorporate every minute detail, both good and bad, into His judgment. If a person is to be brought to trial before a mortal king of flesh and blood surely he will be filled with a great fear and seek ways to escape an unfavorable verdict. What then should he do when he is brought to trial before the Universal Judge, in whose Hands lies the power of forgiveness? Certainly, it would be wise for him to rouse himself from his stupor and do teshuvah before he is pronounced guilty.[36]

Therefore, it would be appropriate for anyone who fears the Lord to make the Days of Teshuvah, the period before the verdicts are sealed, a time for reflection. He should restrict his business activity, concentrating instead on examining his ways. And he shoud occupy himself with returning through teshuvah, because this is the period during which He is most willing to accept teshuvah (see end of Chapter 3).

It should be noted, however, that although the Holy Blessed One is merciful, He only forgives transgressions between a person and the Omnipresent. If someone transgresses against another person he must pacify and appease that person, by word and by deed, before he is forgiven by Hashem. The Talmud tells us (Yoma 85b):

> Rabbi Elazar the son of Azariah expounded: "It is written, From all your sins before God shall you be cleansed (Vayikra 16:30).
> "Yom Kippur atones for the transgressions of a person of the

---

36. As it is written, What shall we do for our sister on the day she is spoken for? (Shir Hashirim 8:8).

47

Omnipresent. Yom Kippur does not atone for the transgressions of a person against his fellow unless he appeases him first."

The Talmud goes on to elaborate on the extent of this obligation (Yoma 87a):

> *Rabbi Yitzchak said: "Whoever enrages his fellow, even if only with word, should pacify him..."*
> *Rav Chisda said: "And he must pacify him before three separate groups of three people each..."*
> *And if the offended person has died?*
> *Rav Yosef said: "He must assemble ten people and stand alongside the grave of the offended person. Then he must say: 'I have sinned to God, the Lord of Yisrael, and to this person whom I have injured.'"*
> *Rav Yirmiyahu had a quarrel with Rav Aba. He went and sat on Rav Aba's doorstep when the maid was emptying out dirty water. Some droplets of the water fell on his head.*
> *He said: "I have been made as a rubbish heap. I need no longer stay here, for I have been forgiven, as it is written, From the rubbish heap He lifts up the pauper (Tehillim 113:7)."*
> *Rav Aba heard of this and went out to greet him...*
> *Whenever Rav Zeira had a quarrel with someone he would go back and forth in front of that person, making himself available for that person to come and apologize...*

Although someone who offends his fellow should appease him immediately, no matter what time of the year it is, he must never delay doing so beyond Yom Kippur. Even if he does not have the opportunity to appease him fully before Yom Kippur he should at least apologize. The offended person should accept the apology immediately, and in turn, Hashem will forgive him for his sins. The Talmud tells us (Nedarim 55a):

> *Rava had a quarrel with Rav Yosef. On the day before Yom Kippur, he decided to visit Rav Yosef and smooth it over. When he came to Rav Yosef's house, he found the servant preparing to blend a cup of wine for rav Yosef.*

Rava said to the servant: "Hand me the cup and let me blend the wine for Rav Yosef."

Rav Yosef was blind and did not see Rava, but when he tasted the wine, he said: "This wine tastes like one of Rava's blends."

Rava spoke up: "Indeed, it was I that blended the wine."

Rav Yosef said to him: "Do not take a seat until you explain these verses to me. What is the meaning of that which is written, And from the desert to Matanah, and from Matanah to Nachaliel, and from Nachaliel to Bamos, and from Bamos to the valley (Bamidbar 21:18-20)?"

Rava replied: "If a person lets himself become as a desert that is trampled underfoot the Torah is given to him as a present, as is intimated in the Hebrew meaning of that which is written, And from the desert to Matanah (Ibid.).

Once he receives the Torah as a present, the Lord gives it to him as a birthright to pass on to his children, as is intimated in the Hebrew meaning of that which is written, And from Matanah to Nachaliel (Ibid.).

If, however, he becomes arrogant in his new-found greatness, the Holy Blessed One humbles him, as is intimated in the Hebrew meaning of that which is written, And from Bamos to the valley (Ibid.).

"Still, if he returns through teshuvah the Holy Blessed One raises him up again, as is intimated in that which is written, Every valley shall be raised up (Yeshayahu 40:4)."

Elsewhere, the Talmud mentions that Yom Kippur is a time for reconciliation (Yoma 87a):

Rav had a quarrel with a certain butcher. Twelve months went by, and the butcher did not come to apologize. The day before Yom Kippur arrived, and still he had not come. Rav decided to go to him instead.

Rav Huna met him on the way and asked him: "Where is the master going?"

Rav replied: "I am going to pacify such and such person."

Rav Huna remarked: "The master is going to cause a death.'[37]
Rav stood on the doorstep of the butcher's house and called out
to him.

The butcher responded: "Go away! I want nothing to do with
you."

The butcher had been splitting animal skulls. After this exchange the blade of the axe came loose from its shaft and lodged in
his head, killing him.

Rav was once reading a portion from the Torah before Rabi.
Rabbi Chiya entered, and Rav went back to the beginning. Rabbi
Shimeon the son of Rabi came, and he once again started over.
Then Rav Chanina the son of Rav Chana walked in. Rav decided
that he was not required to continue starting over after each interruption in honor of the newcomers. Thus, when Rav Chanina the
son of Rav Chana arrived, he continued to read from the point of
interruption.

Rabbi Chanina the son of Rav Chana was deeply offended. Rav
tried to mollify him for thirteen years, each year coming on the day
before Yom Kippur, but Rabbi Chanina would not accept his
overtures.

Why did Rav do so for thirteen years? Did not Rabbi Yosi the
son of Chanina say: "Whoever seeks the forgiveness of his fellow
need not ask more than three times'?

Rav set stricter standards for himself.

And why didn't Rabbi Chanina accept Rav's apology? Didn't
Rav say: "Whoever acts with forbearance is forgiven all his sins?

Only, Rabbi Chanina had dreamed that he saw Rav suspended
from a palm tree. There is a tradition that such a dream is a sign
that the suspended person will become the head of the yeshiva.
Since Rabbi Chanina was at that time head of the yeshiva he feared
that this boded his death. Therefore, he refused to accept Rav's
apology making it uncomfortable for Rav in the yeshiva in Israel.
Rav Chanina felt that by doing so he could induce Rav to go study
Torah in the schools of Bavel (Babylon).If he were to become head
of the yeshiva there it would not threaten Rabbi Chanina's life.

---

37. [Translator's note: Rashi explains that the butcher would be punished by
death for inconveniencing Rav to come to him when he should have gone to Rav.]

(And so it was. Rav went to Bavel to study Torah, and he became head of the yeshiva.)

Once a person has appeased the people he has offended he can then turn his attention to preparing for a complete atonement on Yom Kippur. It is customary to immerse oneself in the mikveh on the day before Yom Kippur. The source for this custom is in the Midrashic directive to be as pure as the angels of service on Yom Kippur (Pirkei d'Rabbi Eliezer 46). According to the opinion of Rabbi Yitzchak Ibn Giyas, this immersion does not require a berachah since it is by custom rather than by law.

Our Sages have also decreed that the day before Yom Kippur be a feast day to show how happy we are to be approaching the time when we will be cleansed of our sins. The Talmud tells us (Yoma 81b):

> It was taught: Rabbi Chiya the son of Rav from Difti says: "It is written, And you shall torment yourselves on the ninth day of the month (Vayikra 32:23).
> "Do we then fast on the ninth day of Tishrei? Does not the fast of Yom Kippur fall on the tenth day of Tishrei?
> "Only this verse comes to tell you that whoever eats and drinks on the ninth day is considered as if he had fasted on both the ninth and tenth days.

This is because feasting on the ninth day indicates, that although we are awestricken and overwhelmed by Yom Kippur, we rejoice at the prospect of being elevated spiritually by the atonement it brings. The Midrash tells us (Beraishis Rabah 11:4):

> It once happened that the military governor of a city told his servant: "Go, buy me a fish."
> The servant could find only one fish on the market. He offered a golden piece for it. There was a Jewish tailor there who offered two golden pieces for the fish. The servant raised his offer to three golden pieces. The tailor, however, raised his offer to five golden pieces. The servant no longer bid against him, and the tailor took the fish home. The servant then went back and told his master all

that happened.

*The military governor summoned the tailor and said to him:
"What is your occupation?"*

He replied: "I am a tailor."

*The governor asked: "Why did you buy a fish worth but one
golden piece for five golden pieces? Moreover, why did you bid
against my servant who was trying to buy it for me?"*

*The tailor replied: "How could I refuse to buy it even for ten
golden pieces for the festivities of this day before Yom Kippur on
which the Holy Blessed One has directed us to eat and drink? And
we are confident that He will forgive our sins."*

*The governor said: "If so, you have done well." And he bade
him farewell.*

Furthermore, this day of festivity before Yom Kippur the Holy
Blessed One shows His compassion for the Jewish people. For on
the one day of the year that he directed they fast He also directed
that they first fortify themselves by eating and drinking. It is
analogous to a king who had an only son and decreed that he fast
one day. However, when the time arrived, he directed that he first
be fed and given to drink so that he would be able to fast easily.

Furthermore, on every Shabbos and Festival we have feasts for
the sake of Heaven. Yom Kippur is also a holy day, but since it is a
fast day it cannot have the spiritual adornments of the holiday
feast. Therefore, we are required to have these feasts on the day
preceding Yom Kippur.

Others offer an opposite interpretation. They point out that if
someone gorges himself immediately before a fast day, fasting
becomes doubly hard since the body becomes accustomed to com-
fort. In this way, they explain the abovementioned Talmudic state-
ment that whoever eats and drinks on the ninth is considered to
have fasted both the ninth and the tenth. In other words, feasting
on the ninth makes fasting on the tenth doubly hard, as if he had
fasted two days.

Although the fast day of Yom Kippur is itself an atonement for
one's sins, the intelligent person does not wait for Yom Kippur to
do teshuvah. Rather, he prepares himself by doing teshuvah
beforehand.

It is common medical practice that when a doctor sees an improvement arises in a patient's illness he will make sure to empty the patient of any harmful substance that caused the illness. For instance, if a harmful food caused the illness he will give the patient an emetic to cause him to vacate the contents of his stomach. Otherwise, the crisis might kill him.

Yom Kippur is the crisis, the catharsis, of the illness of the soul. If a person enters the crisis still burdened with his sinfulness and transgressions he places himself in jeopardy. He risks an unfavorable verdict. But if he cleanses himself through teshuvah Hashem will purge him of his sins and purify him, as it is written, If your sins shall be as red thread, they shall become as white as the snow (Yeshayahu 1:18).

Therefore, it would be wise for a person to examine his ways carefully, early on the day before Yom Kippur, to repent from his sins and to acknowledge them at the very beginning of the day. Then he should immerse his body to purify it. But more important, he should seek to purify his soul. Let him not be as one who immerses himself while grasping a vermin in his hand. Such an immersion is worthless. Let him prepare to enter this day cleansed and stimulated through teshuvah. Then the Blessed Creator, in His attribute of Mercy, will forgive his sins on the Day of Atonement, as it is written, For on this day will He atone for you, to purify you (Vayikra 16:30).

Chapter Seven

THE DAY OF ATONEMENT

As Yom Kippur begins a person should see to it that his body and soul are sanctified, that he is like a heavenly angel completely free of sin. The Midrash tells us (Pirkei d'Rabbi Eliezer 46):

Samael[38] saw that he could find no sins among the Jewish people. He said: "Master of all Worlds! There is a people on the earth that resembles the angels of service. Just as the angels of service are barefoot, so too are the Jewish people shoeless on Yom Kippur. Just as the angels of service are pure of all sin, so too are the Jewish people pure on Yom Kippur. Just as the angels of service are at peace with each other, so too are the Jewish people at peace with each other on Yom Kippur."

When the Holy Blessed One hears such testimony even from the adversaries of the Jewish people, He forgives them.

The Midrash also tells us (Devarim Rabah 2:36):

When Moshe went up to the Heavens he overheard the angels of service as they were praising the Holy Blessed One, saying: "Blessed is the Name of the Glory of His Kingdom forever and ever."

Moshe brought down this exalted phrase and imparted it to the Jewish people.

There is an analogy to this. A person stole a beautiful ornament from the palace of the king and gave it to his wife. However, he warned her: "Do not adorn yourself with it other than in the privacy of your own house."

---

38. [Translator's note: Samael is another name for the angel of death, the adversary.]

The purpose of this analogy is to explain the custom to say this phrase, "Blessed is the name...," under our breaths throughout the year but to say it aloud on Yom Kippur. The Midrash is telling us that this phrase is actually the property of the angels. If we have appropriated it for our own use we must use it inconspicuously, uttering it only in a whisper. On Yom Kippur, however, we are compared to the angels of service and are entitled to utter it loudly without stealth. This is also the basis of the custom of some people to remain standing through the day of Yom Kippur. Since we are compared to angels we should remain standing as they do.

The day of Yom Kippur falls on a date that is very auspicious for atonement. It is the date on which Avraham circumcized himself, the removal of the foreskin being also a covenant for the removal of the pollution from the heart, the ears, and the lips. it is also the date on which the Jewish people were forgiven the sin of the golden calf-idol and on which they were given the Second Tablets of the Commandments. For these very reasons, our Sages have told us that the girls of Yerushalayim would dress up more lavishly in honor of Yom Kippur than for any other festival (Taanis 26b, Bava Basra 121a).

It can also be said that Yom Kippur falls during this time of the year because during this time there is danger of rebelliousness and disobedience. The summer harvest having just passed, the storehouses are full of grain, fruit and all the bounty of the earth. People have a tendency, at this time, to be caught up in their material abundance. They tend to congratulate themselves for their accomplishment, forgetting that their bounty comes from Hashem. Hashem, therefore, decreed that Yom Kippur come at this time to rouse people from their stupor, to induce them to abandon the pursuit of gratification and their rebellious ways, to induce them to purge their thoughts of all false ideologies. Only by restricting one's physical drives to those necessary to keep body and soul together and for the preservation of the species can one hope to achieve fulfillment as a human being.

Indeed, it is to awaken people to the sinfulness of their being steeped in material pursuits all year that a *chatas* sacrifice of a goat is brought on Rosh Chodesh at the beginning of every month. It is meant to remind us to examine our ways and never to despair of doing teshuvah as long as the soul is entwined with the enemy, the body. (One's physical body is truly one's enemy. It is Satan; it is the evil inclination; it is the angel of death.)

On Yom Kippur, however, *two* goats are brought as *chatas* sacrifices. One of these goats is sacrificed on the altar in the Bais Hamikdash close to Hashem; the other is sent away to be thrown off a hill and dismembered. These two goats represent the two classes of sins and what our attitude should be towards them. It is fitting to take this comprehensive in-depth to sinfulness on Yom Kippur, because it is the appointed time for teshuvah.

The first goat represents those sins that are caused by the physical drives of the body. These are sins of excess, of attaching too much importance to the body which will eventually die and disintegrate. These physical drives should be harnessed instead; these energies should be channeled into the service of Hashem. The body need not be destroyed. It need only to be kept at arm's length and under control. Therefore, the goat representing this class of sin is lifted onto the altar to be sacrificed and brought closer to Hashem. (Similarly, the five abstentions on Yom Kippur are meant to subjugate the five senses and bring them under control.)

The second goat, however, represents the intellectual sins, including foolish ideologies such as the various forms of polytheism in which the gentile nations believe and distortions of those parts of the Torah that are couched in colloquial terms. These attitudes can serve no constructive function in the service of Hashem. They must be destroyed completely, without leaving a trace. Therefore, the goat representing these sins is sent far off, thrown down, and dismembered.

The reason for goats being used for these sacrifices is because the goat is a destructive creature. Thus, by these sacrifices we implore that the Jewish people be protected from the two kinds of harmful influences; we ask that harmful intellectual influences be destroyed completely, and that the harmful physical influences be limited to enable us to serve Hashem properly and for the sake of Heaven.

Chapter Eight

FASTING ON YOM KIPPUR

While it is certainly true that the Holy Blessed One has assured us that the day of Yom Kippur is in itself an atonement for the sins of Yisrael, it is nevertheless necessary for every individual to abandon his sins, to express regret over having committed them, and to resolve never to return to them. Only when combined with teshuvah such as this will Yom Kippur be an atonement. Otherwise it will not. The Talmud tells us (Yoma 85b):

If someone says: "I will sin, and then I will do teshuvah" he is not given the opportunity to do teshuvah.

If he says: "I will sin, and Yom Kippur will atone for me" Yom Kippur will not atone for him.

Yom Kippur atones for transgressions against the Omnipresent. Yom Kippur does not atone for transgressions against another person, until that person is appeased.

Clearly, Yom Kippur atones only for those worthy of atonement.

Moreover, the purpose of fasting on Yom Kippur is not to torment the body while leaving the soul contaminated by sin. The Holy Blessed One detests such fasting and rejects it. The purpose of fasting is to stimulate people to examine their deeds and their ways and to set them to right.

This is the essence of the exchange between the Jewish people and Hashem as recorded by the Prophet. The prophet tells us that the people complained, Why did we fast and You did not see? why did we torment ourselves and You did not acknowledge it? (Yeshayahu 58:3). And the prophet writes that Hashem replied, Behold, on the day of your fast you tend your affairs, and you demand payment from all your debtors. Behold, your fasts are occasions for quarrel and dissension, and for striking with villainous

57

fists, you do not fast on this day to make your voice heard on high. If such is your fast shall I choose to accept it? a day that a person torments himself? is it just to bow his head like a reed and to spread out sackcloth and ashes? do you call this a fast day and a day of appeasement for God? Rather such is the kind of fast that I choose to accept, it is to break open the chains of villainy, to loosen the bonds of oppression, to set the downtrodden free, to uproot all oppression. Rather it is to distribute your bread to the hungry, and to bring the wretched poor into your house, when you see an unclad man that you clothe him, and that from your kinfolk you do not conceal yourself. Then your light shall burst forth like the morning star and your healing shall come speedily, and your charity shall go before you, the Glory of God shall enfold you. Then you shall call and God will answer you, you shall cry out and He will say, I am here (Yeshayahu 58:3-9).

Indeed the Pesikta tells us that a combination of prayer, charity and teshuvah symbolized by fasting most effectively dispels an evil decree (Piska 30).

It is important to note that although we do not partake of physical pleasures on Yom Kippur it is nevertheless a holy day and must be honored inasmuch as Shabbos and the festivals are honored. The Talmud suggests that we adorn this day with beautiful clothing (Shabbos 119a).

As to the liturgy and readings on Yom Kippur, we read the portions of the Torah describing the various sacrifices. We also review the entire order of the Yom Kippur service. The Talmud tells us that when we do so Hashem considers it as if we have brought the sacrifices in the Bais Hamikdash, and He forgives all our sins (Taanis 27b, Megillah 31b). We also read the portion of the Torah listing all the adulterous and incestuous relationships, because many people are guilty of these, either by actual deed or by licentious thought. For the Haftorah we read the prophecy of Yonah so that we can take example from the full teshuvah that the people of Nineveh did, even thought they were not Jewish. The value of their teshuvah is underscored by the mention of it among the prophecies.[39]

_____

39. Our Sages have also instituted the practice of referring to the teshuvah of

At the close of Yom Kippur it is the custom to say seven times: "Hashem, He is the Lord!" Afterwards the shofar is blown. It is said in the name of Rabbi Yehudah Gaon that we do so to symbolize that on this holy day the Divine Presence rests in the lower world among the Jewish people, but at night it rises above the seven heavens and returns to the Upper World. The blowing of the shofar emphasizes this ascension, as it is written, The Lord ascends amidst the teruah... (Tehillim 47:6). We find a similar connection at Mount Sinai, as it is written, When the trumpet sounds they may go up on the mount (Shemos 19:13), and our Sages explained that this signified the departure of the Divine Presence (Mechilta Yisro).

We find mention in the responsa of the Geonim, in the name of Rav Hai Gaon, that it is customary to blow the shofar after Yom Kippur is over but that it is not obligatory; it is only a symbol of the yovail year or to confuse Satan.

We can also venture another significance. After Yom Kippur has atoned for us our souls are freed from the shackles of physical bondage. In fact, even our bodies have been purified and are worthy of eternal freedom. Therefore, we blow the shofar to symbolize our future liberation which will be to accompaniment of the shofar, as it is written, And it shall be on that day a great shofar shall be blown... (Yeshayahu 27:13).

---

the people of Nineveh among the words of contrition spoken on a special fast day called because of a calamity (Taanis 16a). We say: "Our brothers! Sackcloth and fast days are not in themselves effective, only teshuvah and good deeds. For thus do we find the case with the people of Nineveh. It is not written of them that the Lord saw their sackcloth and their fast days. Rather, it is written, And the Lord saw their deeds... (Yonah 3:10)."

Menoras Hamaor excerpts available from
the Yeshiva of the Telshe Alumni:

The Merits of Giving
The Days of Awe